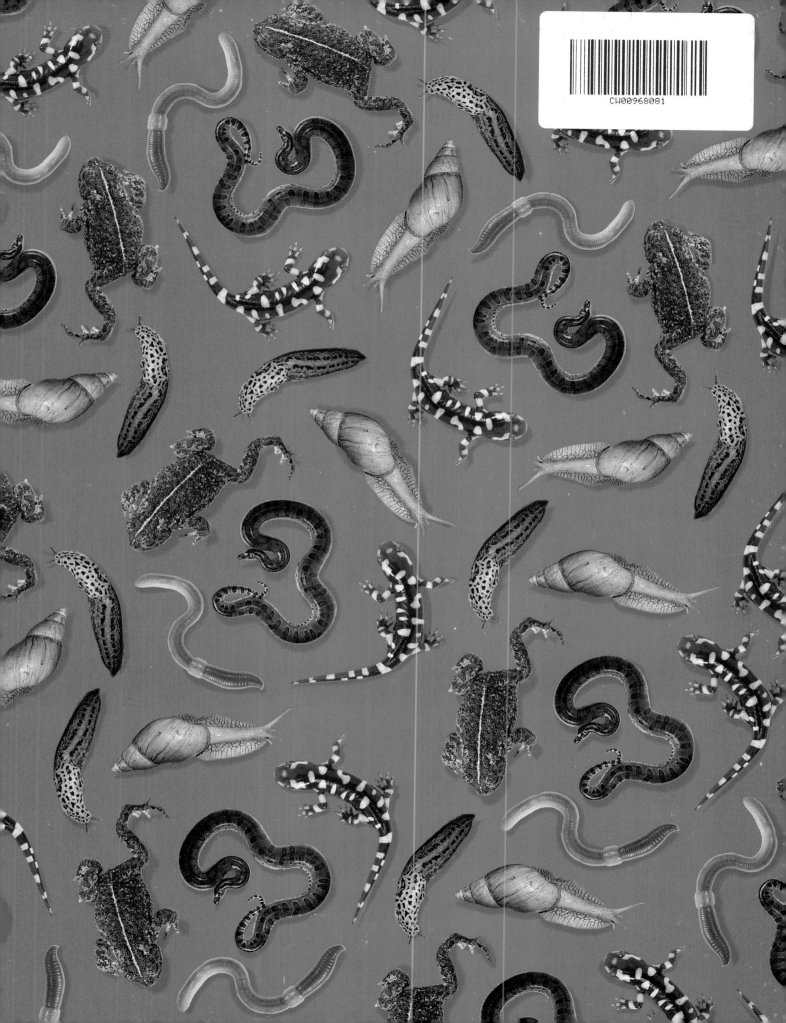

A DORLING KINDERSLEY BOOK

Project Editor Mary Atkinson
Designers Karen Lieberman,
Anna Benckert

Deputy Managing Editor Mary Ling
Senior Art Editor Jane Horne

Production David Hyde
Picture Research Ingrid Nilsson

**Photography, at risk to life and
limb, by** Frank Greenaway
and Kim Taylor

Additional photography by
Geoff Brightling, Neil Fletcher, Mike Linley,
Tim Ridley, Jerry Young

First published in Great Britain in 1996
by Dorling Kindersley Limited,
9 Henrietta Street, London WC2E 8PS

ISBN: 0-7513-5462-7

Colour reproduction by Colourscan
Printed in Italy by L.E.G.O.

The publisher would like to thank the
following for their kind permission to
reproduce their photographs:

t top, b bottom, l left, r right, c centre

Bruce Coleman/Jane Burton 12/13c, 12cl/MPL
Fogden 11br; Premaphotos endpapers,
4tl, 5cr, 10/11c, 12bl, 12/13bc, 13br

THE REALLY South Gosforth 1st School HORRIBLE HORNY TOAD

AND OTHER COLD, CLAMMY CREATURES

THERESA GREENAWAY

DK

A DORLING KINDERSLEY BOOK
London • New York • Stuttgart • Moscow

UGLY PRINCES

Most toads have clammy, warty skin in mottled colours that help them to sneak up on prey and hide from enemies. Many also use poison as a back-up defence.

Toads squirt their poison from glands behind their eyes.

A horned toad will lunge at an attacker, biting as hard as it can.

A mouse fits easily into this toad's large mouth, but swallowing it is trickier.

Horned toads hide among leaves and wait for prey to pass by.

Ornate horned toad

When threatened, common toads stand on their toes and puff up their bodies.

Common toad

The cane toad is one of the largest in the world. It can grow as big as a Frisbee.

Cane toad

Although a cane toad can produce 30,000 eggs at a time, most of its young don't make it to adulthood.

The poisons from some toads have been used to make antibiotic medicines for treating animals and humans.

Some toads try to escape capture by urinating. This makes them lighter, helping them leap away.

Chilean red-spotted toad

LITTLE LEAPERS

Many shiny rainforest frogs use powerful chemicals to keep their enemies at bay. The most famous are poison-dart frogs. They produce some of the most lethal toxins known.

Poison-dart frogs come from South America, while mantellas are found only in Madagascar, yet both are colourful and poisonous.

Poison-dart frog

Bright colours warn enemies of the lethal toxins in these frogs' skin.

The deadliest poison-dart frog has enough poison in its skin to kill almost 1,000 people.

Poison-dart frogs

There are more than 50 different types of poison-dart frogs.

Some poison-dart frogs and mantellas are so lethal that you must wear thick gloves just to touch them.

Golden mantella

Many mantella frogs are just as deadly as poison-dart frogs.

Green and black mantella

Mantella

Frogs can use their colours to identify other frogs of the same species.

A frog's slippery, slimy skin makes it hard for predators to grab hold of it.

Green mantella

Native South Americans used to tip arrows with the toxins from poison-dart frogs.

Sticky toes help frogs climb and grip.

OOZING ALONG

Slugs may look like gooey blobs, but without their slime they'd never survive. They need it to move and to keep their bodies moist. It also repels birds because it's so sticky.

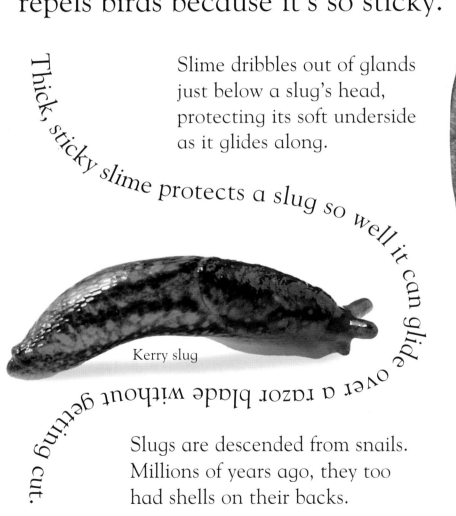

Slime dribbles out of glands just below a slug's head, protecting its soft underside as it glides along.

Thick, sticky slime protects a slug so well it can glide over a razor blade without getting cut.

Kerry slug

Slugs are descended from snails. Millions of years ago, they too had shells on their backs.

Brown rainforest slug

Brown slug

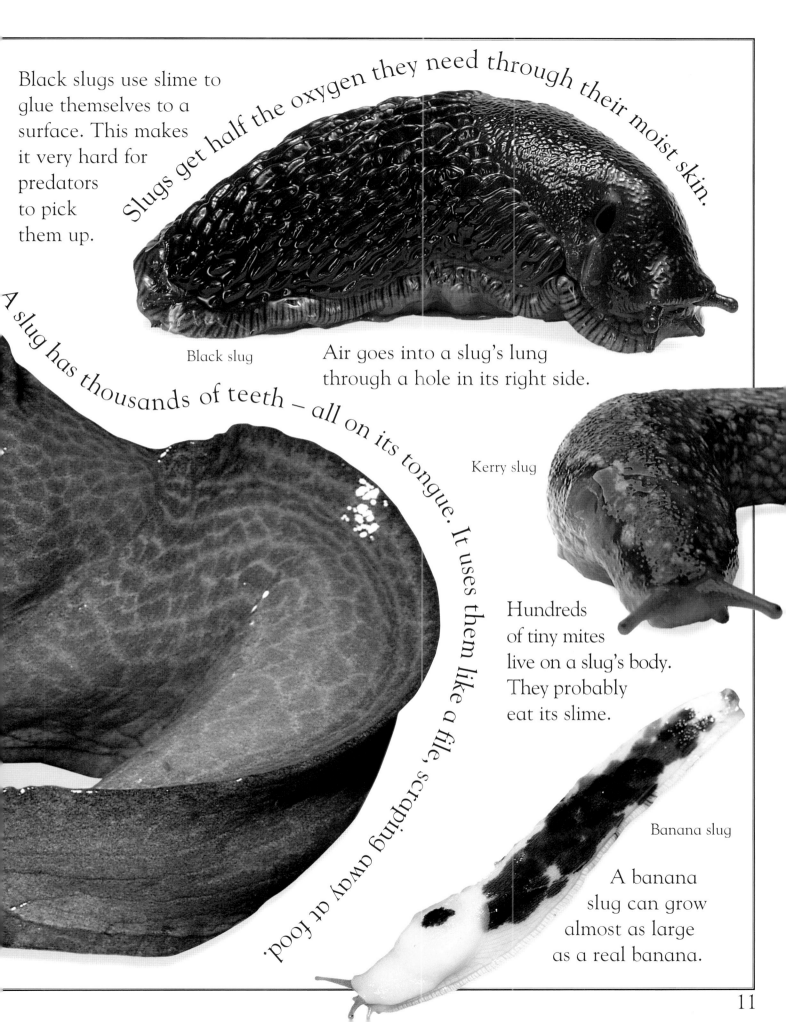

Black slugs use slime to glue themselves to a surface. This makes it very hard for predators to pick them up.

Slugs get half the oxygen they need through their moist skin.

Black slug

Air goes into a slug's lung through a hole in its right side.

A slug has thousands of teeth – all on its tongue. It uses them like a file, scraping away at food.

Kerry slug

Hundreds of tiny mites live on a slug's body. They probably eat its slime.

Banana slug

A banana slug can grow almost as large as a real banana.

SLIMY TRAILS

A snail's soft body makes a tasty meal for a bird. For protection, snails not only ooze an offensive slime, like slugs, they also retreat into hard, chalky shells whenever danger is near.

Garden snail

Snails have eyes on the ends of their tentacles. If you touch a tentacle, it will quickly shrink back into the snail's head.

White-lipped snail

Giant snail

A snail's shell is made from chalk and protein that is squeezed out of a special place on its back.

Some snails can scare off birds by bubbling out a mass of sticky froth.

African snail

When a garden snail goes into hibernation, it uses slimy mucus to plug up the entrance to its shell.

Garden snails

Imagine the wide, slimy trails they must leave behind as they glide along.

Giant snails really do grow as big as this one.

White-lipped snail

Long plaited door snail

Instead of being either male or female, snails are hermaphrodites, or both sexes.

Snail shells coil around like spiral staircases. Most shells coil clockwise.

SQUIGGLY AND SQUIRMY

Worms have no eyes, no legs, and no bones, yet they still manage to eat, grow, and move around. Like slugs and snails, slime helps them in lots of ways.

Earthworm

Some worms live in water. Peanut worms burrow deep into sand or mud on the seabed.

Earthworms can make different kinds of slime.

One kind of slime is used for moving, and another for mating. Some worms even ooze a stinky slime to ward off enemies.

Earthworms

To move, a worm stretches its head forward, anchors itself with tiny hairs along its body, and then pulls up its back end.

Earthworm

14

Gardeners love to see earthworms because they help stir up the soil and mix nutrients into it.

Earthworm

Earthworm

There are roundworms almost everywhere. Some live in soil, others in plants or animals. Most are harmless, but some can spread diseases.

Peanut worm

These roundworms are parasites. They live in dogs' intestines, eating half-digested dog food. They don't need to look for food, they're surrounded by it.

Some parasitic worms can live inside humans.

Parasitic roundworm

CREEPY CRAWLERS

Caterpillars are little eating machines that grow larger every time they shed their skin. They can't run or fly, but they can protect themselves. Some produce poisons or terrible smells, and others disguise their bodies.

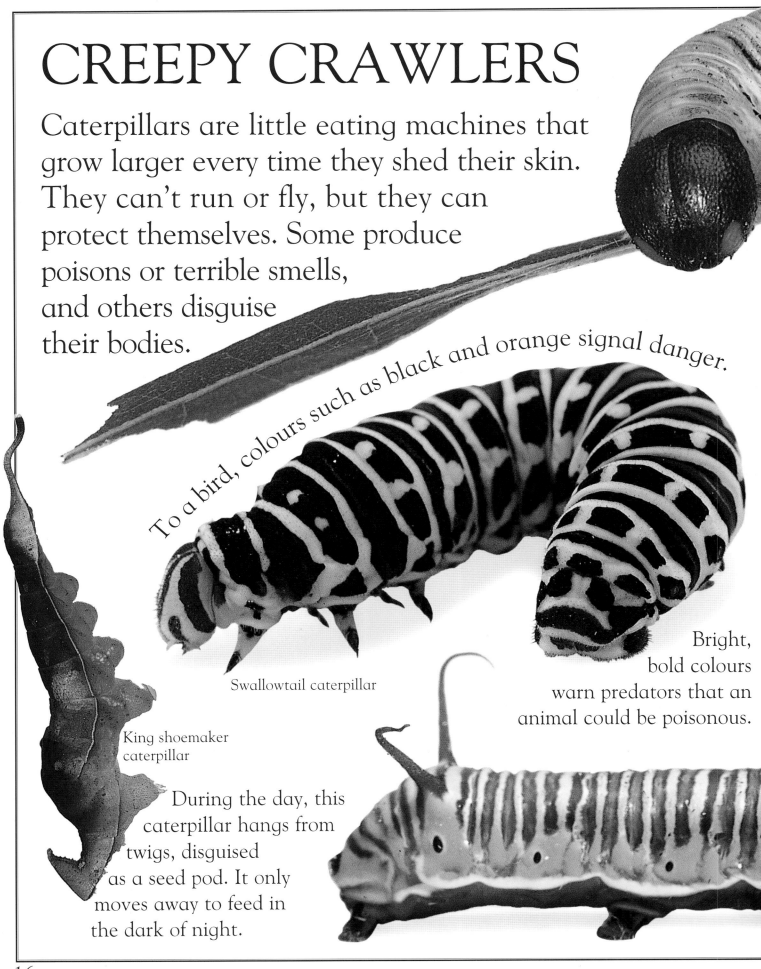

To a bird, colours such as black and orange signal danger.

Swallowtail caterpillar

King shoemaker caterpillar

Bright, bold colours warn predators that an animal could be poisonous.

During the day, this caterpillar hangs from twigs, disguised as a seed pod. It only moves away to feed in the dark of night.

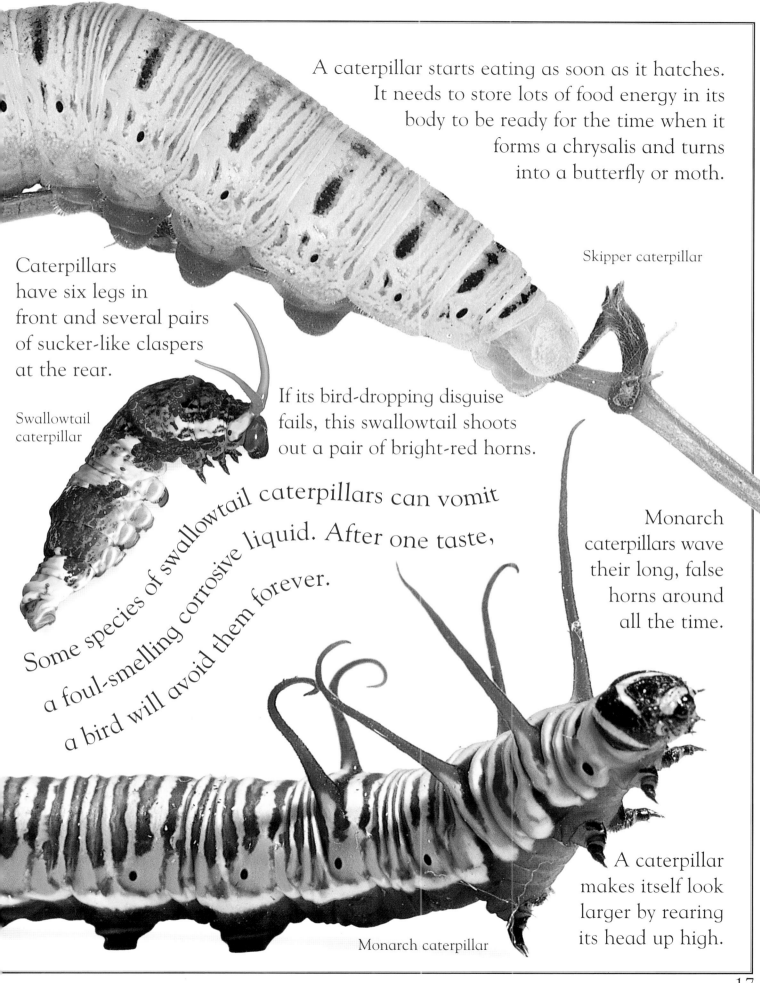

A caterpillar starts eating as soon as it hatches. It needs to store lots of food energy in its body to be ready for the time when it forms a chrysalis and turns into a butterfly or moth.

Skipper caterpillar

Caterpillars have six legs in front and several pairs of sucker-like claspers at the rear.

Swallowtail caterpillar

If its bird-dropping disguise fails, this swallowtail shoots out a pair of bright-red horns.

Some species of swallowtail caterpillars can vomit a foul-smelling corrosive liquid. After one taste, a bird will avoid them forever.

Monarch caterpillars wave their long, false horns around all the time.

A caterpillar makes itself look larger by rearing its head up high.

Monarch caterpillar

17

SLINKY SNAKES

Many people think snakes are cold and slimy, but if you touch one, you'll find it's smooth, dry, and even quite warm. Snakes just look wet because their scales are so shiny.

Flying tree snake

Like many tree-dwelling monkeys, tree snakes can grasp branches with their tails.

Flying tree snake

Flying snakes can't really fly, but they can glide from one tree to another.

Milk snake

This viper's bold pattern camouflages it among dead leaves.

Snakes sneak up on their prey silently and strike quickly. They stab with their long, sharp fangs, injecting a paralysing venom.

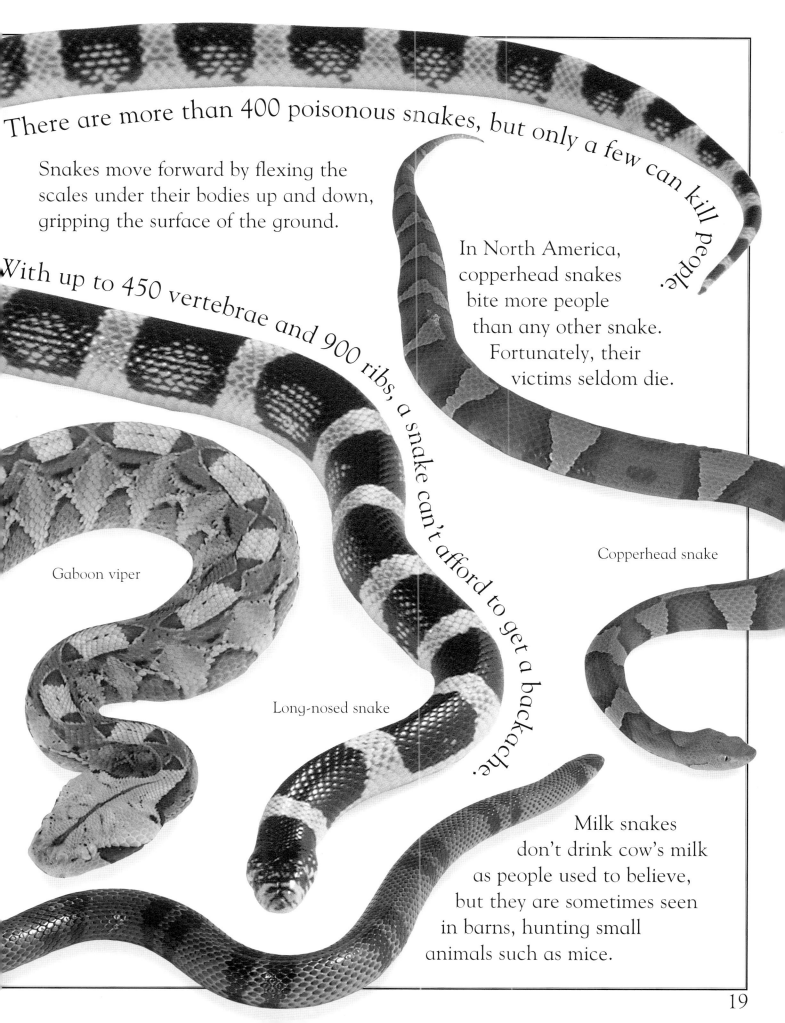

There are more than 400 poisonous snakes, but only a few can kill people.

Snakes move forward by flexing the scales under their bodies up and down, gripping the surface of the ground.

With up to 450 vertebrae and 900 ribs, a snake can't afford to get a backache.

In North America, copperhead snakes bite more people than any other snake. Fortunately, their victims seldom die.

Gaboon viper

Long-nosed snake

Copperhead snake

Milk snakes don't drink cow's milk as people used to believe, but they are sometimes seen in barns, hunting small animals such as mice.

SLIPPERY AND SLITHERY

Like frogs, young newts and salamanders go through a tadpole stage. They live in water and breathe through gills. Later, most species develop lungs and live on land. But even as adults, they must always keep their skin moist and slimy to survive.

Tiger salamander

Land-dwelling salamanders have feet shaped for climbing and digging

Newts and salamanders often eat their own skin after they shed it.

Crested newts hide in dense waterweed during the day, only coming out to feed at night.

Crested newt

Salamanders like fresh meat. In fact, they prefer it alive.

Oriental mandarin salamander

The bright orange spots along this salamander's body are called warts, but they're not real warts, just raised lumps.

Tiger salamanders

Tiger salamanders are the largest salamanders on land. They can grow up to 40 cm long – that's twice as long as a man's hand.

European tree salamanders

Although they look fierce, tiger salamanders hunt only small animals, such as snails and slugs.

If a salamander loses a leg or tail, it will slowly grow another one to replace it.

The bold, bright patterns on these salamanders warn predators that they're unpleasant to eat. Especially bad-tasting chemicals ooze from glands behind their eyes.

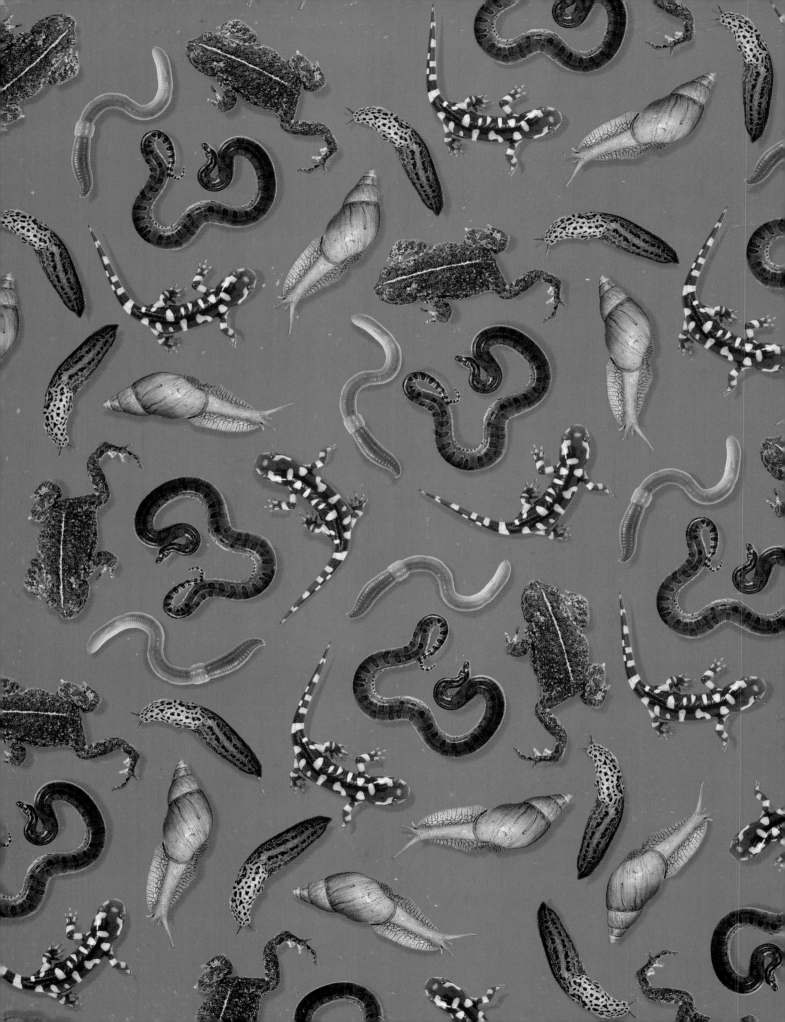